SOMATIC REALITY

Somatic Reality

STANLEY KELEMAN

CENTER PRESS
Berkeley, California

© 1979 by Stanley Keleman

All Rights Reserved
including the right of reproduction
in whole or in part in any form

Published by Center Press
2045 Francisco Street
Berkeley, California 94709

Designed by Eric Jungerman
Production by Hope Emerson Winslow

Typesetting by Accent & Alphabet
Berkeley, California

Library of Congress Catalogue Number: 79-88485

ISBN 0-934320-00-4 hb
ISBN 0-934320-05-5 pb

For my family

And in thanks to Ian J. Grand
who edited this book.

Anatomy is destiny.

SIGMUND FREUD

Man has no body distinct from his soul.

WILLIAM BLAKE

Contents

Preface

In the early part of my life I sought a source of authority, a reference, a philosophy from which I could find the values and purpose that would serve as a conduit for my energies. Many of the values of my culture at that time were unacceptable to me. They were either mechanistic, low level materialism or a pathetic religious dogma that was no longer historically applicable. My feelings of awe and curiosity about the beginnings of things and the nature of existence found no home either in the world of science or in the images of the Orient.

Philosophy did offer me Henri Bergson, whose concept of an *élan vital* struck at the core of an intuition I had had of a kind of energy that sought to be known and experienced. Years later Martin Heidegger's ideas of intentionality and phenomenology also brought more sharply into focus this intuitive grasp of a process of life seeking to be known.

Sigmund Freud's and C. G. Jung's notions of the unconscious as the unknown and as the seat of a psychic energy appealed to me most deeply, although I never surrendered my cosmological notions. My longing for a cosmology found a measure of connection in some of the ideas of W. Reich, who saw this psychological energy as both biological and cosmological. I also had a modest education in the social psychology of Adler, which gave me a sociological perspective.

The notion of energy, as elucidated by Bergson and Freud, led me to pursue the experience that could help me know myself, my world, the nature of living, and to arrive at a path that was satisfying and purposeful. In pursuing this energetic psychological direction I worked with my own body in an attempt to uncover the unconscious and to experience the *élan* directly. Whether I chose to use my mind to observe or free associate, or to use my body as an attempt to intensify my excitement through breathing, or to do exercise meant to loosen the sociological muscle contractions, I was led to a deeper and surprising knowledge of my body. I found that both an intensifying of feeling and image making was a result of these explorations. I began to have a whole range of experiences, which encompassed past and present, ideas and needs, thinking and feeling, urges to act and urges to wait, archetypal pictures and emotions, inner and outer space and time.

I felt at home in this world of many dimensions, but of course this being at home was fraught with anxieties. I thought at the time that the strangeness I experienced was due to the releasing of old conflicts and energies that I had to resolve and become accustomed to. This was in line with then contemporary psychological thought. It was not until much later that I knew that I had stepped outside the realm of our society's knowledge. We had no tradition of living a bodily life. Culturally we were only prepared to suppress the body and force a world view of the life of the mind on ourselves.

After a while I realized that the concepts of energy and body were dualistic and polarized just like the older notions of mind and body, spirit and matter. These dialectical interplays felt uncomfortable to me. I felt that I did not inhabit my body, I *was* my body, that I was not a polar opposite to what was material. My experiments had led me to quite another sense of myself. I was not unconscious and impulsively acting out; I had a sense of myself and felt that I could have a distance from events. But this was only one aspect of my functioning. I had many ways of knowing myself and the world around me, only one of which was distance making. Some were empathetic and participatory knowings that gave rise to a feeling of oneness. Others were of an emotional resonance in a vision I shared with others. I had a continuum of experiences.

I felt and knew, in an emotional flash that lit up

my cortex and fired my muscles, that I, my life, was a continuum of diverse experiences, from cellular to social. And these events were linked, connected in a pattern of continuity that had form and that sought to form. For me I had found my frame of reference, my own *élan vital*, my energetic cosmological source. It was in the experiencing of myself as a somatic continuum of experiences that had a tending, a predictability, an urge toward form, toward forming. The old notions of body and mind no longer had meaning. The culture had made the body inferior to the mind, feelings less than reason. But I realized that organismic experience was a territory more vast. Previously to talk about the body one had to settle for physiology, kinesiology or psychological, symbolic imagery linked to myth or anthropological reconstructions. I began to employ the notion of somatic process to imply that our biological process was more inclusive and complex than we had believed and that it was something we knew little about.

Somatic reality is the universal forming of experience, the history and present tending toward more satisfying living. Our somatizing is the way we connect to our history, to others, and to the cosmos. To partake of this reality is to gain satisfaction, pleasure and a felt frame of reference.

This book is to lay a framework for somatic living.

Introduction

Our times are represented by a confusion about how to live. Modern forms of rationality have desecrated our emotional lives, and we have discovered that the fulfillment of an idea, an ideal, is not necessarily emotionally satisfying. We have neglected our emotional reality, and the source of our self-nourishment: our bodies.

Our psychology and modern philosophy have not gone far enough. Having weakened the shibboleths, the "thou shalt nots", they have been unable to tell us what, then, we *shall* do. They have given us a theory of behavior that does not tell us how to live a biological life, and they have not presented us with a philosophy or a physiology that helps people know how to grow and find satisfaction in the emerging shapes of their own bodies. Instead they have intellectualized the physical, making it seem that if we change our minds through insight, our bodies will follow.

Insight can be important, but to know is not

enough. To alter your life situation is to be able to change your function. This is not merely to change your mind, but to change the way you use yourself. To change your mind is to change your body, to function differently. To change your mind is to change the shape of yourself. Psychology has not presented either an image of life as a biological process of continual reorganization or an understanding of this process that would enable us to adequately deal with the changing shapes of our lives.

Most of us live out our lives according to an image we have of the universe or nature or the social milieu, copying beliefs and patterns of action enforced by family, schooling, or the media. We have virtually no sense of the subjective aspect of our inner physical being, on which our whole experience is based.

But we, as subjects, as biological process, can be and are a source of real knowledge. Our bodies give rise to the impulses, visions, codes, and societies that we live and that make our lives and relationships possible. Out of this biological ground comes the meaning that we know as our lives. "Man has no Body distinct from his Soul," wrote William Blake, but we continue to describe man in the old ways of mechanical science.

Anatomy is destiny. Freud said that in 1912 when he said that our bodies are our fate. How despairingly true that must have been for him, and for millions of others of his time, and to a great extent for all of us. For it says so clearly that the anatomical structures of our bodies, our bodily limitation, our sexual differentiation, spell out the destiny of our experiences. But those people who work with the body, like osteopaths, chiropractors, yoga teachers, physiotherapists, Rolfers, bioenergetics practitioners, and others, have established several important facts. One is that the body is more plastic and mobile and reorganizable than we think, and that the body is capable of regenerating, reshaping, and growing. A second is that a person is capable of participating in these changes, not only on a biochemical level, but also in terms of the shape and motility of the body; that is, on the muscular neural level. The body speaks the language of change and may learn to reorganize for pleasure and survival.

Rembrandt, the painter, in his self-portraits, kept a pictorial journal of the history of his life. To my knowledge, nobody has created such an extensive series of images that reveals the impact of the body's formative process and clearly shows the development of human emotion. However, there is more to be grasped from this panorama of self-images from adolescence to death, and that is the different bodies or shapes that Rembrandt had in his life: from the flamboyant young man to the dense and deeply emotional adult, his feminine side, and the picture of frailty near his death, where he is the mischievous magician waning home. Clearly, Rembrandt revealed, for everyone to see, who he had become during the course of his life, how he formed himself, and how his life experiences formed him.

The transfiguration one sees is not a trip from youth to decay at all, but a journey through the different types of bodies that formed the life of this man. It is like a tree that has an extended history, every year growing new leaves and flowers, every year adding a new ring of growth. Or like the life of a rose bush: each season new roses, new bodies spring up and bloom, then wilt and die, but the life of the rose bush goes on. In the same way, we also live the bodies of childhood, of adolescence, of young adulthood, of maturity, and then we die. We are different people throughout our lives: the worker, the lover, the parent, the thinker, the athlete. And each of these has a different body that goes through transitions and transformations. Connections change, our loving changes, satisfactions and desires change, goals and images change. There are marriages, separations, changes of careers, and the death of loved ones. All of these changes require learning new behaviors, and reorganizing actions and responses.

In this book, I have tried to develop both a philosophy and methodology of re-organization that can enable persons to participate in the transitions of their lives by experiencing their own biological process. This book is concerned with how we organize our excitation, feeling, behavior and relationships somatically, and how we can learn to reorganize them. It teaches how we can recognize and live with the emotions and processes that accompany the calls for change we experience, in ourselves and in our surroundings. Throughout the book, there are somatic exercises that can be employed to train yourself in your own self-formation, that can teach you about how you can conduct your life and how you can alter it.

It is my experience and belief that learning to live from our own somatic process enables us to find a source of continually deepening meaning and satisfaction.

I

Somatic Organization

A man's state of mind at any given moment becomes apparent in his way of being present, his behavior and his gestures.

Man, as a Person embracing body and soul, develops and realizes himself in every gesture he makes.

KARLFRIED, GRAF VON DURCKHEIM

The Human Being
as Somatic Process

A NEW VISION

*A*T THIS stage in the evolution of society, our psychology and philosophy of man stand in the same place, I believe, in which Newton stood in relation to Einstein. Man is described in ways linked to the old physics: man as an object, man as a robot with a spirit, man as a mind/body dualism, as a mechanistic accident. But man is not a machine with a mind or with a spirit. He is a complex biological process that has many realms of living and experiencing.

When we conceive of ourselves as a living process, we can talk about the aspects that we see as part of our living functioning: thinking, feeling, gesture, satisfaction, sexuality, dependency, individuality, community, love, and inner vision. Then we see that our organismic life, our life process is the ongoing orchestration of a multiplicity of events. And we are struck by the fact that from these events we form a unity, a direction, a cohesive life that continually shapes and reshapes itself in the many realms of its functioning.

One of the outstanding facts about biological process is that we continually change our shape. Life builds form constantly. This is clearly illustrated by our embryological development, in which we form our infant bodies through a series of events. First from egg and sperm, we form a multiple-celled organism, then a creative being with only a rudimentary nervous system, and then a fetus with arms and legs and a recognizable human form. Finally we are a fully formed human infant. This same process of making and changing bodily form continues throughout life. If you have a picture album, and see over a period of thirty to forty years the images of yourself, you will grasp the notion that you have had many bodies in your life.

The somatic life is the life of the child, the adolescent and the adult. These are separate lives connected by memory through an enduring nervous system. We have the ability to form many bodies, selves, personalities, and to have many lives in our lifetime: like a plant that keeps flowering every season in a year, a plant with different bodies. We have a public body and a private body, a rational one and a non-rational one. When we can experience our lives like this, we can begin to appreciate the miracle of the life of our body, of our biological process.

There is what I call the long body. That body is the present history of all the bodies we have lived, from the egg-sperm implosion, through all the embryonic stages, through childhood to the present. This body keeps elongating itself throughout our life. But our past lifestyles can still be seen in the present shape of our bodies. The history of our past emotional satisfactions and dissatisfactions leaves its mark. If, for example, we have lived a competitive life, the scars of competition, like raised shoulders and fighting upper-chest breathing, may still be present.

How we can transit from one body image, a lifestyle, to another, speaks of the life of the body as it continues to grow, and holds a mystery, a well of deep joy. But most of us are educated to recognize ourselves by a static image or role, and we say, "that's me; that image is me; that body stands as me." We are forced too early, I believe, into roles that are identifiable and acceptable. And we acquire these roles, these bodies, by something we do to ourselves. We create action patterns which match that image of what we think we should be, and then identify with the action pattern we have created.

In this way, we may begin to think that we have a body which must obey us. We establish some mythical "I" and believe we no longer have to experience ourselves as a biological process. When this occurs, we lose the sense of the body that we are, and the body we live; we lose touch with the forming of ourselves and think of ourselves as bodies and minds.

In the transition from any one body to another come the crises, the difficult stresses that reveal or make problems. Most of us do not know how to help these outgrowings become a new self. We tend to think of our maturity as a state of mind rather than a state of the body, and we do not know how to help the organism mature.

Because we have little understanding of our own biological process, we often experience ourselves as victims to the ongoing urge of the life of the body to shape itself anew. Because we have not been educated in how to live and participate in the emotional upwellings, the changing desires and the developing hungers of our life process, we often look upon the transitions of our life with dread. We miss the opportunities that are presented to us by our ability to change and form.

In trying to understand the life of the body, it is important to understand the steps in the human process. What are the steps in the process of our body forms, of our lifestyle? What are the steps that we go through in changing our minds, our bodies, and how do we go through the transitions from one lifestyle to another—from the body of a youngster to that of an adult, from the lifestyle of a competitive hunter to that of a cooperative family member?

24

It is important that you identify with the process of your own transitions. How have you affected your own change or been victim to the processes which forced you to change? And how can you participate in the process of self-formation, permitting growth to occur with you taking an active part?

If you look back at your life, you find a series of high points and low points — "that I liked," and "that I avoided," something there and something here, something fresh and something dim, and then a sense of duration. And if you look closer, you see those things that not only attracted you, but moved you in a certain direction and taught you things. Those events were your teachers, not in a moral sense, but in what actions were evoked or repressed. "I stopped laughing then." "Here I became serious." "Here I learned to imagine." "Here I learned to lie." "Here I learned shame." "There I found distrust."

The way in which you have accumulated information and experience and shaped yourself into a piece of behavior, how you have done it, becomes the secret to how you help yourself grow. In how you learn is the secret of how you unlearn. It is in how we learned to do things that the real answers of how to reorganize ourselves lie.

Let me give you an example of what I mean. If you write down on a piece of paper the events of your life connected with a particular emotional reality, you will begin to notice a pattern of connection, a developing pattern of shapes that are linked. If you are afraid of authorities, for example, then write down the first instance of this fear, and then others, with parents or teachers. You will begin to get a grasp of the progression: first there is parental disapproval, then perhaps peer humiliation, or browbeating in school or feeling inadequate. Perhaps there is a fear of doctors, or police, or of your boss.

The next step is to experience the bodily connections that these images and memories have. There is a bodily shape, a configuration of feelings, a way of standing toward the parent or teacher or boss. You can begin to see the effect these events have had on the tensions of your body, how you have shaped yourself, the kinds of feelings you have expressed, and the feelings you have avoided. Maybe you can feel how you adopted a cringing attitude, or became a good boy or a good girl by avoiding the feelings of anger. Perhaps you have developed chronically spastic musculature, deadened the feelings of assertion, tightened your throat so that you wouldn't talk back. In this way, you can begin to learn how you have shaped yourself. This becomes the key to experiencing the process of your own formation. In learning how you have formed yourself in response to life situations, you are enabled to rework the way you use yourself.

The person who is capable of understanding his process is capable of being in situations appropriately or relativistically, not in a stereotyped way. This gives the opportunity not only to experience the actual situation he is in, instead of his image of it, but to shape himself and the situation; i.e., to make his world. This frees him from being stuck in behavior that is obsolete for his survival. He can give it up, leave it, and reformulate the nature of his actions and images, based upon the nature of his experience.

Through this book, you can educate yourself in the perception of your process and in its language, be it emotional or in the form of urges, images or feelings, and to experience your thoughts, feelings, and actions as bodily events that are muscular, visceral. In this way, you will be able to learn and translate your experiences into a new way of using yourself.

Experiencing our process teaches us how we learn to change our bodies and how this becomes a lifestyle. Being with the process of how we change and form, creates excitement, challenge and satisfaction. There is risk, but that risk adds zest to life rather than distress. We are part of a living process in which our subjective experiences have a lot of weight in how we form and shape our life. Growing is an attempt to introduce experiences about the nature of living which can help free us from concepts and feelings that no longer apply. It is an attempt to give room for your feelings to express themselves in the nature of new images, for new possibilities to find expression in the present rather than living out outmoded world views. In doing this, you can learn to sustain those internal states that give you the feelings which make life enjoyable, as well as create those values which have been the ongoing drama of all individuals.

My hope is that this book can help people live from their biological process so that they can create their own life, generate their own values and see change as a part of the living. The reward is an emotional deepening and a broader spectrum of satisfaction.

The Life of the Body

HOW WE SHAPE
EXCITATION AND FEELING

*I*N ORDER to understand the idea that we make our bodies by the way we live, it is necessary to understand the basic life process of excitement, and how we shape it. The body is a river of events and images, the stream of our goings on—our thinking, feeling, action, desiring, imagining, a current of motility. This current of tissue metabolism which constantly shapes and reshapes itself as our bodies we can call excitement.

Excitement is the basis of experience. It is knowledge, information. Excitement is the basic pulse of life. It flows up in a burst of illumination, it retreats to re-charge. The body is an ocean of biological excitement, manifested as urges and desires, generating new shapes and movements toward satisfaction. How we live it tells us about how we shape our lives.

All of our various feeling states represent different shapes of excitement, different densities and intensities. Excitation has qualities and tones —soft, hard, gentle, irritating, brittle or firm. We categorize these different qualities, heighten these feelings, and then express them as emotions. For example, an aggregate of feelings comes together and we develop the emotion we call love, which is composed of lust, desires, caring, tenderness, warmth or joy; or another aggregate of feelings we call anger, which may be composed of arrogance, irritability, shouting, or striking. All of us recognize and respond to these different patterns of excitement.

How we choose to let our excitement expand and grow, how we choose to express or not express it, reveals us. Many of us have an investment in dulling ourselves to never show being excited, either from deep disappointments or fears of being foolish. We can recognize the kinds of excitement people live by the shape of their bodies and the gestures they form. Where there is too much restraint, there is a boundness as if the world must be constantly warded off; they look musclebound. People with these bodies do not allow their excitement to expand and grow, living in patterns of continual constriction, they keep their energy constricted, reaching out as little as possible; they are over-orderly and over-restrictive. People with no restraints or weak boundaries are victims, surrendering to every impulse. They have shapes that are weak, and toneless, like warm jello. And generally they have developed patterns of explosion, in which they permit their bodies the catharsis of impulsively unloading excitement, like children instantly acting out all needs and feelings. In short, one kind of person has a weak container, the other an overly rigid container. One pushes life down, one lets his process leak out, erupt. One compresses himself, presses life in; the other expels life.

If one is neither too bounded nor too un-bounded, the steps of his own process of excitement begin to be contained, and a direction, or organization of feeling emerges. One experiences one's own inner law, one's own inner formative process, one's own self-organizing, one's own life direction.

One of the most common patterns today of non-participation, of resistance to the self-organizing of excitement, is what's called the "explosive" style, the actor-outer. In the past, it was the depressive, the rigid one, the chap who over-controls himself, super-independent, the over-private person, the inner-actor.

The explosive style has become a very popular if misguided approach to satisfaction, be it for power or pleasure, replacing the rigid type, the over-controlled person. For the explosive person destructuring is impulsive. Both explosive and rigid folk fear not feeling alive, but the explosive people handle this by erupting. There is little joy and very little trust in these life processes. This pattern of excitement may be a response to unmet needs, or to high stimulation from the environment, or to an innate high-energy level whose expression is somehow inhibited. Whatever its origins, it presents a functional inability to contain excitement.

The urge to express excitement impulsively is a natural urge in children, but as we mature, we become more and more able to contain and extend excitement, we become increasingly able to hold gently, to love deeply. People who habitually erupt, who constantly explode, are people who have not formed a personal structure that will contain and expand their excitement. Consequently, they are unable or unwilling to feel themselves or to form their lives. They do not allow their excitement to grow into feelings; instead they act at the level of sensation, the level of peripheral, external excitability—in short, they live an unbounded life. They use others to give them a skin, a sense of themselves. They are like a stew always boiling. A basic characteristic is an explosive overactive, overdoing, or a depressedness with fits of eruption. While the overbounded person curtails his excitement, always avoiding externalization, the explosive person shrinks the human dimension to provide a relief from excitement.

Whether we are involved in stiffening or unbounding ourselves, we often take the attitude that "this is the only way", or "this is the answer". This self-righteous attitude rationalizes both our compulsion to express ourselves and the violence that we do to ourselves. We try to dominate ourselves this way; we manipulate ourselves by judging, by criticism. We try to prevent ourselves from changing, from allowing ourselves to reorganize, by developing rigid bodies or unbounded ones. We stiffen ourselves until we no longer respond emotionally, or we explode until we are exhausted. Laurel and Hardy are good examples: the overbounded broomstick, and the underbounded clown.

Our attachment to activity, our style of excitation, usually stems from fear of collapse, failure, or dread of helpless instability. We fear the heights and depths of our own excitement. Above all, we abhor the open-ended pulse of our formative process, which includes feelings of powerlessness as well as feelings of power, instability, security, emptiness, fullness and wholeness. We want power, we want potency, but we will not risk even momentary powerlessness for the sake of contacting the power inherent in our own formative process.

The important thing to recognize is how one lets excitement arouse one's body and in what form: how one lets excitement go through him; how one permits or prohibits oneself to be excited;

and how one lets oneself be excited with others and with oneself. One way to do this is to keep a history of the path of your own excitement. Simply note, day by day, the ways you have handled your excitement in various situations, with your spouse, or friends, at work or while walking down the street. You will soon begin to see a pattern to the ways you have permitted or re-stricted your excitement in different areas of your life and in different areas of your body. You may begin to perceive how you perpetuate a particular level of feeling and expression. You may be able to see that excitement calls forth feeling responses. These feelings, whether negative or positive, love or hate, spread to fill us, to expand us. They connect us to others, link our thought and action, and also make life passionate.

But so many of us have stopped our emotional growth so early that we are frightened of the spontaneity or the impulsiveness of behavior we believe our feelings will lead to. When feelings begin to rise up for many people, they feel they won't be able to do anything, that they will be victim to the feeling. Most of us constructed a lot of self-reliance on our ability to suppress our feelings—not crying, suppressing being angry, hiding laughter, concealing needfulness. We feel our real strength in being able to compress our-selves dead, pretending no feeling and separating ourselves from others.

This is understandable when we look back at the history of our excitatory life. Early feeling is tied directly to the expression of need, be it for contact or nourishment. How these are satisfied or responded to provokes either frustrated kinds of feelings or loving kinds of feelings. If we feel hungry, we need to be responded to; if we need physicality, we need to be touched. Children who don't get what they need begin to feel victimized by their own feelings. The child who needs to be responded to and can't get the parent to respond, or the child who needs approval and can't get approval, begins to experience feelings as dangerous. When a child feels sad and his crying is unnecessarily ridiculed, he begins to feel sadness as his enemy. Or if he's punished for his independent feelings, then he gets to know that these feelings are dangerous. When a child learns he is punished for crying, for anger, for seeking warmth, for laughter, then his readiness to touch, etc., are identified as an enemy. That is, those feelings and those actions become signals that we learn are dangerous. We begin to construct an image of feelings as dangerous and institute a series of bodily patterns that attempt to suppress our feeling or channel it in another direction.

When we have a readiness to be assertive, we may generate internal images, pictures in our heads that we will get punished, tied up to patterns of shrinking or lifting our shoulders to lock in our heads. When we have a readiness to act lovingly or a readiness to act angrily, we may also develop a concomitant protective pattern based upon experience that we will be rejected. So we generate muscular attitudes of shrinking or contracting ourselves to protect ourselves from rejection.

As you trace the pathway of your excitation, you can begin to identify the feelings that emerge. These feelings may be loneliness, sadness, anger, sexuality, or longing for contact, and they may provoke fear, discomfort or dislike. Once you have begun to identify them, you can begin to experience how you try to avoid and control those feelings. What is it that you muscularly do to keep those feelings "under control" in public, or within yourself? Do you squeeze your throat, grab your fingers, compress your chest, tighten your abdomen to deny being vulnerable there?

By following your excitation, you can also begin to experience that there is a particular level of intensity at which you begin the physical attempts to control a particular feeling. Perhaps you will begin to get an understanding of the fear that is embodied in these physical actions such as, "I am afraid that when I want to reach out for affection, I will be rejected. If I express my anger, everyone will leave me, or I will be humiliated."

Feelings seek response. If one is crying, one is not only crying to relieve the pressure of the situation, but because one wants a response from the world. When we become aware of what our feelings are aimed at, who they are aimed at, and what kind of response we want, we can begin in another way, to live with them. When we begin to see which of those feelings we are frightened of, and at what point in intensity, we can begin to know how we are frightened, how we generate our fear muscularly, and how we generate the images that provoke us to feel frightened. We are then enabled to work with ourselves in a way that can bring us the ability to live with different qualities of feeling and excitement.

I worked with somebody who at a certain level of excitement was overwhelmed. Whatever excitement mounted, he was in danger of being swept away, overwhelmed and over-emotional. He felt he became passive to his feelings and victimized. When he described how he overwhelmed himself, he could identify that level of excitation where he could tolerate the feeling of sadness. Beyond that level he began to be out of control. The sadness that the excitement brought unbounded him. He began to shake, a movement like a sobbing; and he then became a victim, began to lose muscular coordination and the ability to hold back his emotion. There was a certain place where he could have the feeling and then a certain place where excitement mounted and he began to be uncoordinated and overwhelmed. I suggested that he go up to the point at which he could bear the feeling of being sad or glad or excited. Then when he began to recognize the signs of being swept away, to institute muscular contractions that would inhibit the excitement just a little bit, so he could live with this feeling and not be destroyed by it. Then he was able to escalate it a little bit and learn to live with that; then to be able to pull back.

In experiencing your own excitation you may find that you have to tighten your throat if you haven't learned how to turn your feeling of screaming into the feeling of protesting verbally. Or you have to learn how to let tears begin to flow in statements of sympathy or in statements of what you have lost, or to feel the sadness without hysterically sobbing on one side, and being tight-throated and tight-chested on the other. You can learn to use the muscular pattern of your getting ready to cry, to actually cry, or to express the sadness verbally, saying "I am sad", or to recognize you don't have to cry. You can protest, and pull back from the screaming. In this way, you can begin to develop the spectrum of your feeling expressions. In doing or working with these things, you will begin to see that the process of feeling is many-dimensional. It may be love and hate, grief and laughter, desire and disgust, or love and aggression.

We have many feelings and they may be in conflict with each other. We can feel sad and angry at the same time. We can want to be friendly and guarded; we can want to reach out to touch and hit simultaneously. A way to experience this is first to feel the complexity of actions and the complexity of feelings, to see where they are located in your body—the anger in the hands, the sadness in the chest, the clinging or hitting in the fingers. Then let that part of the body complete the action. Clench the fist and reach out, lift the chest and put the chest down, let the pelvis reach out sexually, let the jaw look angry. Allow the whole organism to express the different feelings and the different action patterns.

Learning to move parts of your body as an expression of sadness or anger will be a form of dialogue by which you can then help yourself live with your feelings. You will find that conflict is not a problem only. It is a source of richness. Being able to live with mixed emotions and mixed feelings is an art, expressing our complexity.

Another dimension of the emotional life you will discover as you continue your exploration of excitement and feeling is that feelings are meant not only to evoke responses from other people, but also to keep people at a distance. So you could ask yourself, how do the feelings that I am having distance people or bring them closer?

How one creates distance and how one creates closeness become very important in understanding how one lives with sadness, gladness, joy, or despair. You can begin to see whether the excitation, the feelings are heading toward being including or excluding. Do you want to be part of, or do you want to be outside of? Can you be distant without feeling abandoned? Can you be included without giving up your individuality? Feelings mean to be inclusive in certain situations, but they should not mean to make you a servant. Distinguishing that difference becomes very important.

Perhaps you will begin to experience that you attempt to distance people by withdrawing into yourself, pulling in your shoulders, squeezing your chest instead of asking them to leave or leaving yourself. You may want to retreat, but always feel an obligation to stay, accompanied by concomitant feelings of frustration, anger or helplessness. Or when you begin to feel close with someone or intimate, you may find that you are stiffening yourself. As your desire for contact increases, you may institute a pattern of holding yourself bodily, accompanied by fears of being overwhelmed, rejected, or ignored. You may find yourself overexciting yourself or stilling your excitement as you desire to come close or as you desire to withdraw.

Here again, once you have learned the pattern of your own responses, you can begin to rework them if you are inclined to do so. You could, for example, begin to ask people to leave when you want to be alone, or permit yourself to withdraw when you have had enough contact. You can begin to soften yourself somewhat as you get closer to someone. Perhaps you can allow more excitement, or permit yourself to be less explosive or cathartic.

In talking about how we shape ourselves, what should become clear is that we are capable of living many levels of feeling and excitation. One can react to one's feelings by grasping, holding, not letting go, like squeezing a fist, "I am not going to let this feeling go", like penny-pinching, or a desperate attempt to control the feelings from embarrassing or overwhelming oneself. Or one can explosively erupt with feelings, act them out, never to be in control of oneself. But we are also capable of keeping our feelings inside us without compressing or squeezing, to contain them, and allow them to move us toward pleasure and satisfaction.

Being able to contain ourselves, to live our somatic life, gives us the opportunity to learn how excitement and feeling build up and satisfy themselves. We can learn to allow the readiness of action to sustain itself until we are ready to act appropriately. Experiencing how we shape excitation and feeling teaches us that we can participate with ourselves rather than over-control ourselves. We can learn what self-expression is and what self-management is, and not have fixed images of how we should satisfy ourselves or what will satisfy us. We learn that self-expression is finding those modes of acting which build our lives and give us meaning and pleasure.

The How of Behavior

LEARNING THE SOMATIC WAY

OF SELF-FORMATION

IN THE last chapter, I talked about the organization of excitation and feeling. Now we turn to a discussion of the somatic organization of behavior.

The brain and muscle system and the inner organs are capable of being educated through experience, and they are then capable of stereotyping behavior and of repeating forever what has been learned. If we have learned in the past to inhibit inner pulsations, then that is what we continue to enact. But our bodies are also capable of relearning. If we feel our bodies, the process of how we have learned to do things, what is lived, then we can change it, reorganize ourselves, and teach ourselves anew. The challenge is to be with the feeling of formation, the feeling of how we shape ourselves in relation to events and in relation to other people, and to seize this opportunity to change patterns of self-usage if previous stereotypes are no longer satisfying.

What is crucial and generally forgotten by the very nature of the stereotyping process is that each person, in growing up, has had to create, practice and perfect patterns of expression and social behavior. We are told, "Don't be needy, don't be sad, don't be impatient"; that we have to learn to control ourselves. But what we do to ourselves to carry out someone else's ideas of good behavior may be to inhibit our peristaltic, intestinal movements, interfere with the rhythm of the heart and blood vessels, or contract the skeletal musculature. These actions prevent the enacting of impulses to reach out, run or make noise.

In her book, *The Attitude Theory of Emotions,* Nina Bull, a teacher of mine, described emotional expression as a three-part sequence. First there is a genetically inherited organismic pattern, then a preparation for action and finally the action itself. In crying, for example, there is first the genetic pattern, then the readiness to cry and then the crying. The first and earliest stage of this pattern is hardly knowable in a conscious state. The second stage is quite perceivable. When a child gets ready to cry, it first holds its breath, it ends a particular breathing pattern, screws up its face, twitches its mouth, opens its mouth and cries. In an adult, before crying starts, you will notice how deep and focused the sadness gets. This second stage is important to recognize because it is shaped and influenced in terms of developmental events. A child who is screamed at, rejected, or hit, develops a stance of readiness to defend itself, or a pattern of fearing rejection, not as just a mind memory, but as an emotional muscular brain set. The muscles are tense, ready to act. What is developed is a structured readiness to respond in a particular way to certain environmental cues.

Throughout life we continue to learn organismically. In sexual arousal, for example, we develop a pattern of enacting our sexual behavior based upon our experiences, thereby constructing an organismic attitude toward sexuality. In school we learn to shape a particular pattern of learning and curiosity, to develop certain patterns of readiness to respond to questions, authorities and information. In work, we adopt and perfect particular organismic patterns that we believe to be important for our effectiveness and survival, be it subordination or dominance, shrinking or controlling. I would say it is a matter of great importance to recognize these patterns, and I have discovered that there is a simple process that can be employed to experience them. In this process, you simply ask yourself, "How am I doing what I am doing?", and allow the questioning to lead you step by step through the layers of your somatic functioning in a given situation. "How" is a request to ourselves to try to discover the order in events.

Suppose we ask a person who is angry, "How are you angry?" He says, "I am angry by screaming." Then we ask, "How are you screaming?", and he may reply, "I lift my chest up and tighten my throat." Then we may ask, "How do you know that?", and he may reply, "Well, I remember it as a kid, so I keep doing that. It's in the feeling of knowing myself." Then you may ask, "Do you know how you got your chest up?", and he says, "I remember as a kid my father screamed at me. I froze and my shoulders went up. Now I see the internal pattern of raising my chest to yell."

How do we get angry? What is the organization of our being angry? Maybe we don't like the way a person looks or what they say to us. But, we have to ask *how*, how do we perceive that somatically? If we feel that people are physically restraining us, trying to stop us, how do we have that image? Are we remembering a time when that happened? How do we make that image? Do we squeeze our eyes, hold our breath? What do we feel in our bodies, in our arms? Do we feel any muscular contraction, any muscular readiness to hit or brace?

Or how do we control ourselves when we are angry? Is there any thought connected to the movement in our bodies or our hands? Is it triggered by a need to touch, ask, or a violation of our time? What is the pattern of our anger? These are sensations that we respond to that are not only in our head, but are motor patterns that have thinking, acting, and visceral components. When we are angry, for example, how do we give ourselves the command to contract and hold our arms at our side? How do we use the image of past experiences in the present? What are the sensations, the gestures we are responding to?

The exercise of *How?* takes us from cerebral attention to organismic perception, from dimly perceived bodily doings toward clarity. We can recognize how we mobilize ourselves to do something, how we enter into that state of readiness to act, how we keep ourselves mobilized.

There are no answers to the question "How?". The answers are in the responses. Our experience is the answer. We can learn something about how we give ourselves the chain of command, how we move our body from one position to another, what happens when we bring one state to an end and learn to begin another. This exercise is the developing of a pattern of experiential alertness. Asking the question "How?" leads us to the discovery about the connection of action patterns that can be disengaged and changed.

This is an exercise, a training of ourselves in the process of recognizing that words and images are connected to muscular patterns, that the body speaks and that fantasy is preparation for action. There is a circuitry of action patterns in us that connects muscle spindles and nerve fibers. We can stop it if we are dissatisfied; and we can start it. We can try on new patterns, accept the old or call for participation with our own organism.

Try it with any event in your life: How do you leave the house each morning? Is there a hurried or worrisome feeling? But then, how do I make myself worried? By thinking of the future. How do I do that? By making pictures or rehearsing the situation or remembering past feeling states and how I handled them or avoided them. Then I see my need to perform. How do I perform? By gritting my teeth, sucking up my stomach. And how do I do that? I recall that is the way I handled my feeling when I was hungry and no one came. How did I do that? I just knew how as a child. How did I know? And at this point, there can be a nonverbal event that speaks in the silent language of somatic process in which there is a profound self-recognition and self-knowing.

How do we do this, how are we doing that? The events themselves speak. Like a dream that reveals itself, step by step, asking *how?* opens the door to the sequence of our doing. How do you get into a fight with your wife? What are the feelings you react to, the inner pictures? How do you shape your responses? What are the steps in the escalation of hostility?

The *How?* exercise teaches the recognition of feelings of self-organization, the phases of the readiness to act, the images and the emerging patterns. These exercises and experiences in learning can be enormously useful to us if we pay attention. For example, when you say to yourself, "I want to extend my pleasure in lovemaking", how do you go about doing that? There is an idea that you want to extend your pleasure. You have read about it or someone has told you about it, now how do you go from images to action, from idea to satisfaction? The place to begin is with what you are doing rather than trying to impose a way of doing that is different. Once you perceive how you try to control escalating sexual sensations, for example, or how you have not been able to handle your partner's moving aggressiveness, how you enact that muscularly, you are then in a position to bring that behavior to an end. Do you cramp your belly, pull up your guts, or create a ring of tension around the root of your penis to control your excitement? Do you go blank or limp, become helpless, sponge up the excitement of your partner by pressing heavily on them? Do you start a compulsive flow of images by squeezing your brains so you don't feel in the chest or genitals? How do you make yourself feel helpless? Is it the idea that you will be helpless or that you are beginning to actually feel uncoordinated in different parts of your body? Maybe your breathing isn't in phase with the movements of your pelvis, or your pelvis is moving too fast for your breathing. Or maybe you have ideas of failure which make you breathe too quickly so you can't feel sensations. Or maybe you have the idea that you have to satisfy your partner by moving very quickly and strongly.

In these ways you can experience how you are doing something. Perhaps you are making yourself impotent or frigid. Since this is how you do it, how do you stop doing it? But that question has to a great extent been answered by itself. When you feel yourself breathing too quickly or moving too quickly, you understand immediately that maybe there is a way to slow down. You tell yourself to slow down through a verbal command or an image, and then invoke certain movements which slow you down, using the same movements as before.

Now we have two parts to our exercise in learning. The first part is the recognition of a present action pattern. The second is using the pattern that has been recognized to form another action pattern, a new forming. This holds true for any of the patterns you have discovered in learning and want to change.

Take one of the patterns that you recognize. Let's say you do this by setting your jaw and semi-clenching your hands into a modified fist. To end this pattern, you can finish the action by clenching your hand to make a fist. You can get a feeling of the pattern of action by completing it, or by exaggerating what you are doing. This way, you notice the different degrees of contraction in the pattern. Or you can go the other way, from clenching the fist to extending the fingers, to open the palm and experience the elongation which is the destructuring of clenching, through a continuum of relaxing to form a pattern of open-handedness.

Any pattern that you discover can be used in this way; you can go to the extreme, to finish the action—only slowly—or you can extend it the other way. In this way, you can train yourself to recognize the sensations of the continuum of muscular-emotional coordination. You experience your muscular pattern, and through this learning are enabled to discover other alternatives.

This process of going through the full range of muscular, emotional pattern, I call the accordion. The accordion is the range of possibilities, the continuum of action, the marks on the ruler of expression. Actions and gestures can be rehearsed, through extension and contraction, backward and forward through an action pattern, like an accordion player. When we reach out, we see that we can reach out half way, halfheartedly, or committedly, all the way, a quarter of the way, one-eighth of the way. There are many levels of emotional nuance in reaching out, all sorts of muscular discrimination, of commitments and actions. How we prevent ourselves from total reaching is as important as the reaching itself. By learning this, we can begin to help ourselves to change our emotional distress patterns.

Both the *How?* exercise and the accordion can be further used to identify the social roles you construct in social interactions. This is done in the following way. Either in an actual social situation, or in imagining one, you can begin by asking yourself how you have organized yourself somatically. You may, for example, find yourself with your chest sunken, your throat constricted, and your pelvis pulled up. There may be little feeling in the legs and genitals. Whatever pattern you discover is then exaggerated by contacting the muscles involved more strongly. If your chest is squeezed you squeeze it more, if your shoulders are raised you raise them higher. You make a somatic caricature of the pattern and then attempt to identify both the feelings that accompany this organization and the image that it creates. In this way you can begin to identify the social role you enact somatically, i.e., the good boy, the victim, the little girl, the concerned helper.

Or, conversely, you may first notice that in social interactions you are constantly mischievous, seductive, arrogant or placating. You can then use the *How?* exercise to discover how you create this role, this attitude, somatically. In either case, once you have the feeling of how you are organizing a pattern somatically, you employ the accordion.

You experience the different feelings and qualities that accompany degrees of tension and relaxation in various parts of your body. In doing this you engage in a kind of bio-drama, experiencing and experimenting with a variety of possible roles and feelings of yourself. And you are enabled thereby to develop somatic organizations that can give you richer and more satisfying social interactions. This, of course, is what I mean by constructing our somatic reality.

The other aspect of the organizing process that is important to experience is the dimension of time. Sequence is not only a spatial event, it has duration and repetition. Duration is the heart of process. How long does a sexual desire last, or hunger for touch, or pain? The recognition of duration opens the door to time as a flexible, living event, rather than a programmed ideal.

There are three basic kinds of time that we can learn to recognize: First there is the distinction between my time and their time. My time means the time I need to assimilate, the internal time I need to learn something, to gain satisfaction. Their time means environmental time, society's time, the external time in which we are expected to respond, the time we are measured by, the pressure we are under to perform a task, do a job and then be judged dumb, bright, quick or indolent. Then there is the time which emerges as shared time, the forged rhythms that are neither wholly ideal nor wholly mine.

At the basis of most human dilemmas is the struggle for time: how long does it take to do something? What do we do when someone else is not ready for us? Many of us experience stress or dis-stress, because we are not doing things in our own time. We cannot meet their time demands and ours are frustrated. We are either trying to slow ourselves down or speed ourselves up, to avoid a job or perform a job. Avoidance takes as much energy as performance, and in either case, the proper flow of our own time is interrupted. Conflict occurs when somebody wants us to move faster or slower than we want to move.

Conflicts in learning arise from the imposing of another's speed on one's own assimilating speed. For most people, education and social adaptation is the imposing of public time on our time, the overriding of individual rhythm and process by public process, narrowing more and more our own individualistic pulses. There may be discrepancies of frequency between lovers, or employers who protest the slow pace of workers paid by the hour.

Many behavioral problems, like sexual dissat-isfaction, are problems of time, and much of our illness comes from distorting our own rhythms. We eat too fast and we get sick. We take too long to respond to anger and there are severe cramps inside of us. Today even our cellular life is altered by mood drugs and alcohol, which speed us up or slow us down. The sense of natural rhythm and growing sequences is lost and we become confused about the pattern of our own hungers.

Here again, the process of *How?* can be enormously useful: Make a list. In the left-hand column you can write, "my time", and in the right-hand column, "their time". On the left-hand column write, "private self", and on the right-hand column, write "public self". Then you can ask yourself what time do I take for myself and what time do I give others? What do I recognize as doing things for myself, how do I recognize doing things for others? How much time do I give for the unfolding of my needs, my own way of making love, my own method of washing the dishes? And how much time do I give to winning the approval of others, my teacher, my boss, my lover, my parents? Asking yourself these questions can reveal where there is conflict or how you have developed the relationship between your time and theirs. If you feel dominated or victimized, it is probably because you haven't permitted yourself enough of your own time. The social self has dominated the private self, and the private self has atrophied. Or the reverse may be true, you may feel lonely and alienated and hungry for contact or approval.

The next step is to begin to question the way

you have constructed time somatically. What muscular patterns do you invoke to slow yourself down or speed yourself up? How do you squeeze yourself to enact the intellectual time demanded by schooling? With what sense of time do you eat, make love, walk down the street, drive on the freeway? How do you do this in your guts, your genitals, your brain, your heart?

I had a client who could not permit so-called wasted time. His body was overbounded; he had a ramrod spine, a stiff, thick neck, a tight, grim look, and overtight muscles. This somatic organization was his attempt to compress time, compress himself, to never let things end, and to not allow himself to go from one activity to another. I helped him to feel how tight he was by putting my hand on his muscles and helped him to learn to end this overbounded state. Then his longing for contact and his fear emerged—his horrendous fear of his longing going on forever, never ending. He resolved his compulsiveness by learning how to wait without fear, by relaxing his muscle panic pattern, and by learning that his infant time was not his adult time. In transferring this learning to his relationship with his wife, he proved to himself that his basic fear of being disappointed was wrong, that he could take his own time and that she would respond in a very accepting way.

When we begin to feel our way of shaping time, we become aware that in our lives we experience many kinds of time: religious, institutional, emotional, biochemical, personal and public. Somatic life is the time of my process, with myself, with others, with the universe. Time determines the relationship of me and my community. When we learn about our own rhythms, pulsations, our own time laws, then and only then do we grasp the essence of real freedom.

Everybody's time is different. Everybody lives at many different times. Appreciating this can do a tremendous amount toward reducing interpersonal stress and conflict. When we realize that other people understand and think thr... gh a problem at a different rate than we do, the rate of excitement in our parent or boss or love builds and ends differently than ours, then we can begin to form relationships in which we harmonize our times.

When we begin to be sensitive to the time it takes somebody to do something, then we can change the way we relate to each other. We can create a shared time, and then withdraw to our own time, and even when necessary operate on somebody else's time.

Once we have begun to establish our sense of how we organize time in a particular activity, we can employ the accordion. We can speed up the activity or slow it down by degrees, increments of 10%, 30%, 70%, 90%. We can move back and forth between what we imagine their time to be and what we imagine our time to be. We can see how much pleasure and feeling occur in different rates of rhythm, and how we can create different kinds of time.

How? is a process meant to lead you deeper into your physicality; it is an emotional muscular function. When this process is pursued, it shows that intimacy and contact have a variety of shapes and times. The *How?* exercise can teach you how you get ready to do something, how long it takes and how you actually do it. What are the muscle patterns? Are there other ways to do it? How are you glum? How are you serious? Do you know how you prevent yourself from being excited, happy, satisfied, discovering what is not enough?

This "paying attention" is to let experiences make themselves felt, not to observe in a way that inspects, looks at, judges or criticizes. This process awareness does not make us observers, but rather self-experiencers, self-empathizers. It connects cognitively, emotionally and physically. It teaches us connectedness, wholeness. To discover *"How?"* is how we can change ourselves.

II

Somatic Transitions

'Letting go' requires not only that we relinquish those imaginings that have determined our understanding in the past, but also the behavior that corresponds to them.

KARLFRIED, GRAF VON DURCKHEIM

Or we could say that desire without a distinct materialization is synonomous with unfulfillment.

WILLIAM BLAKE

The Process of Somatic Transition

*L*IFE IS a series of transitions through which a person has the opportunity to reshape himself, to reorganize his life. But many people do not or cannot make transitions well. These turning points require the learning of new living skills and the building of entire new body habits. Many folks get sick with these crises and changes because they do not have the necessary help, or a knowledge of somatic reorganization.

In the not so distant past, the pace of living was much slower. There were fewer reorganizations demanded in life, and the rituals of birth, the rites of passage and the prescribed litanies of mourning were sufficient to help people through major life changes. But today, changes come at a truly cataclysmic rate, and we require different understandings to be prepared to work through them. Without this kind of understanding and preparation, new situations and demands become

overwhelming and the person ends up emotionally truncated and distressed.

Most of us are ill-prepared today to deal with
transitions except to adopt the hero's stance or the
victim's pose, because we do not have a language
and a method to deal with somatic changes. The
language of psychology has been the language of
insight, but not the language of muscular and
organic change. I am proposing a way of teaching
ourselves the somatic process by which we organize and reorganize ourselves.

In trying to understand the somatic process of
transition, I have been led to the observation that
any life change, be it the formation of a new lifestyle, a separation, a death in the family, goes
through three distinct phases. I call these stages
endings, middle ground and the stage of formation. Each has a distinct set of emotional qualities,
bodily sensations and problems to be solved. The
sequence of change involves first an end of
embeddedness in a particular way of doing things,
then a period of being unformed and in flux, and
then a period of trying out new behavior.

The act of ending a situation, an image, a pattern of behavior or form of life, comes from new
input from both inside and outside. It can happen
suddenly, when somebody dies, or by falling in
love or meeting a remarkable person. Or it can
happen gradually, like the end of childhood or
adolescence. When these alterations occur, we

find ourselves in the world globally. This is middle ground, where one may feel lost, overwhelmed. And yet, strangely, there is always a direction that leads us out of middle ground. It can occur by quantum jumps of insight to action; that is, new behavior. We end differentiation, exist in an undifferentiated state, and then we differentiate anew, like a cell. This is how change happens.

All transitions require a period of separating, a time for waiting, and a time for reorganizing new action. These are the phases of all our deepest wishes: an ending of the secretive womb life, incubation; the emergence into the light of our new desires, the stage of tasting, adolescence, testing, confusion, and then the maturation, the adulthood of desires and satisfaction.

Transitions are acts of imagination and image formation. They are acts of freedom, individuality, and self-regulation which can teach participation in the body's changes. They speak of our ability to respond and be sensitive to new patterns, shapes and form.

It is quite possible to train ourselves to recognize the pattern of mental, muscular and organic sensations which accompany life transitions, to become intimate with the biochemical, emotional, physical and experiential statements of the living process. Experiencing ourselves in this way helps us to dismantle old attitudes we no longer need and to participate in self-formation. By using the notions of endings, middle grounds and the stage of formation, we can learn and relearn to participate in the management of our own growing.

The next three chapters detail each of these stages, examining the problems, emotional qualities, sensations and feelings that accompany each.

Endings

SEPARATION AND
WITHDRAWAL AS
ACTS OF CHANGING

*E*NDINGS ARE signals that some part of our lives has outlived its usefulness, that we must change a relationship or behavior, that the pattern of our life is about to reshape itself again. A process of separation and reformation is about to begin. This is not abnormal; it is part of the normal pattern of life and growth. A child withdraws from its mother; we leave a job; someone dies; we take up a new skill or craft.

Endings are an unbounding, an emotional process of distancing, a withdrawing, a self-collecting which begins to increase excitation and feeling. But first there is withdrawing; we either move ourselves physically away in terms of location, or we begin to reduce the energy of our original connection. Endings generate conflict between staying and going. There is a space created, an emptiness, a void in both the objective world and in our emotional and neurological selves.

Endings bring to a close what has been established as sequential and orderly. Relationships undergo changes — for their own internal reasons — and again, we experience the flux and chaos of life, the unbounded energy of raw excitement generating new responses. It is chaotic and it can be frightening. Things aren't the way they were, and we can't continue to behave as we did. As something begins to end, we generally experience unexplained sadness, unfocused excitement, agitation, upsetting physical and emotional symptoms. We can experience anxiety with boundless free energy that won't fit into any of the old pigeonholes.

Very often, sickness is our response and a clue that an ending is occurring: headaches, intestinal difficulties, heart attacks. We are trying to tell ourselves something: "I am uncomfortable, it hurts; it's not good for me anymore, I can't handle the poison you have been giving me, the lifestyle, the relationship, the way you have structured this life of your body. I am giving you this headache to tell you to change something. I am giving you an ulcer to tell you you are not giving me enough time to digest the food. I am giving you low backache to tell you this is not the woman you want to make love to, or that the way you are making love is no longer satisfying."

The actual experience that people have during an ending is generally unstructured. "I'm lost," we say, or "I don't know what is going on," or "I have no source of reference," or "I have all these sensations and feelings that I am just being swept away by them and don't know what to do." We may dismiss these ideas and think, "Oh, I'm going to be all right," but we feel frightened underneath. Unboundings deal with real identity crises, the patterns of self-recognition. The previous life of our body is threatened and invalidated. No wonder we feel frightened.

The peculiarity of the human organism is that it thrives on stability even though there is a perpetual urge toward growth and change. The way that it aims toward stability is to stereotype, to rely on repetitive behavior, giving a margin of predictability and a shape to our identity. This repetitiveness has a consistency in it. It is the way we do things. It is the way we organize our muscles and brains. We become attached to and identified with these patterns of behavior — because they represent survival and pleasure, predictability and ongoingness. As stereotypes and patterns of self-recognition become threatened, we do almost anything to perpetuate them.

The more energy we have invested in a pattern, the more excitation, the more the threat of a loss of identity. So, we could almost say that willingness to change, to let one's identity be flexible, goes along with the willingness to let excitation reach its own conclusion. Endings force us to face the unknown.

Feelings can also be our strength, for the process of survival begins with the ability to respond in an unprogrammed way. When the old structures don't work, we cannot continue to use them; when familiar patterns of behavior become invalid, they must be discarded. If we are to survive and go on to the next stage of our lives, we must first confront situations in a state of emerging helplessness, and not fall back to old automatic responses which have become counter-productive or even destructive. Real wisdom is when we recognize an ending, instead of clinging to delusions that there is safety in habitual static patterns. If we permit our holding on to come to an end, we encourage our potential for new relationships, new bodies.

It is possible of course to get stuck when something ends and refuse to go on. Some people try to remain children or adolescents, to maintain a status quo. Others can be so frightened and resistant that they literally die. Some patterns have become so ritualized and accepted, we become so deeply attached to them, that we feel that to give them up is equal to death. We may be able to dismiss the behavior cognitively, but we still cling to it emotionally.

Many people try to preserve their relationships

at a level at which they have functioned in the past, to avoid transition or crisis. Often we try to prevent transition and crisis because we are frightened that we will not be able to make a relationship work. But it is precisely this attempt to maintain the status quo, in which we engender a readiness not to change things, that causes tremendous distress. It inhibits new interactions, new learning from occurring, slows down process; we become resigned and our emotional processes become sick and dull, the very life of the relationship is drained away. We destroy what we sought to preserve.

Many problems of frigidity or impotence are really statements of not wanting to perform anymore or not wanting to let the events of loving change one. People become frigid. "I don't feel anymore," or "I'm impotent because I don't want to perform." These are statements about being afraid of emotional crisis, or not trusting one's responses which will allow a reshaping of the relationship. Relationships change throughout all of one's life. We have to permit that change to occur to keep deepening our relationship. Our loving experiences reshape us, reshape the way we use ourselves and create the energy that deepens us individually and communally.

When situations come to an end, the willingness to establish a different kind of connection becomes more imperative. The thrust of our movement is to make different contact with ourselves and with others, to make new connections, more feeling for satisfaction.

When we resist change and cannot accept endings, distress is the most common symptom, the most frequent reaction. We begin to thrash about like confused children: "Should I run? Should I placate? Should I fight? Should I investigate?" For example, the woman whose relationship with a man is ending, who doesn't know whether she will collapse or stand up. In the past, she may have had feelings of dependency, she has wanted to have somebody to take care of her, to help support her, to give her ideas and to organize her life for her. Now this is ending and her perceived helplessness is stronger than her urge toward the future. Like many people, she has found herself in a position, in an attitude that has now fallen apart. She is afraid she will seek out a new man to depend upon and repeat a humiliating and self-defeating relationship. What is at stake is how she is going to stand on her own two feet and organize her life more independently. This requires ending the dependency that she has been deeply invested in maintaining.

Finding out how we prevent endings teaches us a great deal about how we live our lives. To do this, it is important to remember that we stereotype not only cognitively, but in the musculature. It is the how of our stereotype which gives shape and image to identity. Trying to end something without contact with how we are immersed in it makes endings more tragic than they need to be.

The *"How?"* exercise can be used to experience both how you have constructed a situation or a relationship and how you are trying to prevent yourself from changing. How have you established your pattern of relating to your spouse? Do you maintain a certain level of feeling or expression? How do you shape that muscularly, spatially? How do you prevent yourself from changing this relationship? What do you do bodily to stop the impulses that are moving you to want something different? Perhaps you will find that you stiffen yourself to freeze the past, contract the muscles of locomotion or of assertion, fix the breathing, squeeze the chest, or stifle the throat.

When we end something or take something away, we create a space. How do we begin to react to the feeling of lack of boundary? When someone dies, quickly or suddenly, many people react with shock and never thaw out or accept the death. They keep the room the same, may even keep talking to the dead person or keep referring to them as if they are still alive. All the spaces remain filled or frozen. They haven't allowed themselves to perceive any inner vacuum or reconstitute their old spatial world. It is important to find out how you are handling the feeling of lack of boundaries, inner space, and changing impulses, bodily.

It is impossible to explore or to grow if we remain bound or rigid. But people fear the unknown, they assume they don't have the behavioral tools to reconstitute themselves in a way that is meaningful for their lives. Deep down in their tissues, they relive and anticipate the fears and pains of past endings. Some people are deeply frightened because in early childhood there were too many changes and too much conflict. They were not able to live with feelings of loss, or despair, and the paradox in early transitions. That is why turning points so often result in sickness. But sickness itself can be treated like an ending.

One of the biggest problems when people are sick is that they don't know how to help themselves get well. I helped a girl who became a woman while going through Hodgkins disease. She needed an operation to remove her spleen. What I did was to help her make the transition, the turning point, from having a spleen to not having one, from being intact to not being intact. I helped her go through the process of self-healing. I asked her to do some very simple things to get through this ending. I said, "Now look, what is coming to an end is you as a particular intact organism. This state of health, this body you had, is at an end, and there is a sickness that you are also trying to bring to an end. The first thing I want you to do is to talk to yourself; your conscious word brain must talk to your non-word part, like you would talk to a child. Tell it you are going to be cut open, that there may be pain, that something is going to be taken out, that you are going to hurt, that the hurt is not going to last too long, that you may be in a state of loneliness in a hospital room all by yourself."

It is important to get out the negative images and to replace them with positive images. So, we went through what it meant for the doctor's hands to go into this woman's body, what it meant for her privacy to be invaded, since she had been afraid and had thought of the doctor's hands entering her as hostile. Then I suggested that she should have images of having warmth in her belly so she would actually help the healing process. "How does it feel not to have a spleen? How are you going to function this way? How does the rest of your body feel without that spleen? How does it feel to have this hole in you? How do you learn to walk differently?" This reorganizing of her image process demanded a change in her bodily stance; her body stiffened in an alert way instead of a fearful one. In this way body and image go together. These are the steps that she learned to manage her images and her feelings in going through this ending, this crisis of surgery. Not all endings are so traumatic, but the process of change and crisis and transition is universal.

It is important to recognize that ending does not necessarily mean obliteration or mutilation;

unbounding doesn't mean severing, forgetting, or throwing everything out the window. Rather it is like committing one's self back to the current of life. Endings are not oblivion. They mean taking a distance, changing a connection.

Think about how you separated yourself from the family. What were the body changes that happened? What did you do? What were the sensations? When did you stop sharing your dreams or intimacy? When did you end your primary dependency with them and begin to set up your private world? Endings create separation. To end particular kinds of emotional ties isn't necessarily to obliterate them. As with the family, bonds can be lengthened and made less dense. But emotional bonds lengthen and may deepen at the same time. We may invest ourselves more into the world by creating long streamers of feeling, from the tribe to the world and then back.

This kind of an ending teaches that closeness can also be at a distance, that feelings — as with our family — do not end, but change form, that we end particular kinds of relationships, particular kinds of roles, but we do not necessarily sever connections altogether.

Remember that unbounding, un-forming and de-structuring are part of the inescapable rhythms of life; that endings take place in the service of survival and the ongoingness of biological being.

To deny this state of ending, to hurl away this excitement, results in an inability or an unwillingness to make the changes necessary for survival and deep emotional satisfaction.

Middle Ground

THE WOMB OF
THE UNBOUNDED SELF

M IDDLE GROUND follows an ending. There is a pause, a swelling, a tremendous flood of mixed emotions, sensations and dreams of the future. It is a transitional phase, a no man's land, the cauldron of our biological process out of which we can form a new connection. This slowing down, this pause in middle ground is like a dream state where there are positive and negative feelings that come out of the shadows, as if being lit by a strobe light. Things are out of sequence and there is no sense of recognizable connectivity.

The middle ground is like an ocean welling up with images, sensations, feelings and needs, each taking its turn on the stage, asking, clamoring for attention, trying itself out in the field of consciousness so we can then use it in the social world. Things aren't rational. Time isn't ordered. Gravity is upside down. Middle grounds are androgynous, bisexual. This realm of our inner world is both masculine and feminine; it is a womb where the newly conceived gestates.

It is what happens at the end of harvest before the new shoots come up — the same deep processes are occurring that happen between inhalation and exhalation, between blossoming and re-blossoming. The middle ground is a receptive and conceiving state; it is both the birth of form and the formless; it is a place where things are begotten and conception itself touches us. Simple levels of organization prepare themselves for more complex levels. From the apparent chaos, things arise. Every organizing process has a middle phase where organization is minimal. It is, in fact, embryogenesis, similar to the process whereby the organs are formed before the organism becomes human.

When hard structure, rules and rituals end, we re-enter the world which we experience as undifferentiated, infinite, and real. In this middle place, this pausing, the rigid patterns of the values we have constructed are lost, and it can be awesome.

Middle ground is the great mythical space, the religious place of the unbounded, the unconditioned, the burning bush of unbounded excitation and creative tumult. It is a place of illumination, of a multitude of possibilities. It can be described as an atmosphere, an intuiting cloud; we have ended something and find ourselves suddenly without boundaries where we know the sweet taste of all that feels eternal. In this place, this middle space, what wants to come out of us we usually call crazy, illogical, unacceptable, irrational, out of sequence, unexpected. We are touched by something sacred.

In middle ground there are extraordinary states which take on a shape different from anything we have known. It is also the place of simple existence. It contains the confusions of everyday living, allows things to be brewed, to be reorganized in a less specialized way that forms a starting ground for new form.

Middle ground is an experience of extreme ordinariness and also of intense vision. One either enjoys the waiting or dreads it, feels the pleasure of his own recharging function or tries to skip through it with compulsive activity and ruminations of the past. Middle ground is an opportunity for a person to steep himself in his existence. Learning to live in its creative sea, one experiences the pull of the past and the thrust toward the future.

When the middle ground is avoided the spontaneous upwelling of passions, of the unrehearsed, is never experienced. But many people fear middle ground because there is less control; feelings and images are dominant, not rationality. Middle ground is hard for those people who cannot stand the inbetween spaces. They want to start doing something right away. If they can't resolve something, or do something right away, they become anxious, angry, or sad, or feel as if they are becoming crazy.

People overeat, oversex, overwork, drink too much — all in an effort to relieve the tensions of middle ground, to deny the changes being felt, to drown out the messages from their interior. There is often the urge to be rid of the abundance of raw energy in middle ground, like children who act out every feeling and impulse. But releasing or discharging this energy is not the same as containing it or building with it.

What has to be learned in the middle ground is how to contain the myriad of sensations, feelings and insights; how to allow out process to reveal the new. A mature organism knows how to inhibit itself, how to stop, how to hold, and how to wait. To be able to pause, wait, or inhibit, is to gain freedom from being the victim of our impulsiveness and stereotyped responses. To inhibit allows us to make use of experience. With an ability to contain our feelings with acceptance of the unbounded state, the middle ground is a pause where experience grows and influences the shape of our new behaviors.

When you allow yourself the images and feelings of middle ground you don't have to let anybody talk you into changing in a particular way. Rather, you can accept for yourself how you are experiencing, what you do with yourself, how you do yourself. This way you don't have to blindly live up to images and models superimposed by external conditions which may be exploitative and demeaning. What is crucial in middle ground is to experience and listen to the varying images of your own process.

There are images that are visual and images that can be described as the configuration that occurs from nerve endings in muscle and bone. The pressure and temperature sensors, eye, ear and visceral nerves constantly send a stream of information, images of space or state of being, that is non-visual and non-verbal. It is important to develop a muscular pattern of readiness to respond to what is present. This stance of readiness to organize our behavior is a most important attitude for going from middle ground into new form. There is inner silence, as if listening for a sound. There are feelings of interest. This middle place, all therapists know, gives rise to insight. Deep and unseen connections are intensified or weakened. Life is immersed in mystery.

Middle ground is the great creative soup originating social form from creative chaos. It is the central moment of turning points, the space where something has ended and something may form. In middle ground bodily process becomes the educator, and those who are able to listen to and learn from themselves can participate in their own restructuring from the inside.

During the process of middle ground, the body speaks a multitude of images, feelings and directions of action. Often these are revealed through dreams. A dream can be the body's way of talking about what is happening on the inside. A dream is a message from the self to the self, in which the internal patterns of energy are revealed in both their present and transitional states. A dream can tell us what is coming to an end and can give us a very clear signal about the middle ground state. It speaks to us from another dimension of our existence. Dreams are part of a series of modulations, of new levels of thinking, feeling and acting that are beginning to integrate themselves into our behavior. A dream or a series of dreams can also be precursors or rehearsals for new behavior patterns. The organism is beginning to organize or mobilize itself toward doing something. The dream is the signal of what is ending and a herald of what is to come out of this mid-point.

Suddenly, in the midst of the chaos of middle ground, something begins to organize itself. New possibilities appear as feelings, movement, images, ideas or dreams. All these indicate a new possibility for the organism to reshape itself, to use itself differently.

Let me give you an example of this from one of my own periods of middle ground: At the time, I already had an extensive background in somatic theory and education, but I was dissatisfied and didn't really know what new direction to take. Then I had a dream about a woman who was watching a man deliver a lecture on how things should be done. All of a sudden, the woman said, "Oh, stop all that talking and lay down. You have got to experience in order to know what I am talking about." She said this to me in a dream, and she got me down on the floor and began in a very rhythmical way to use her hand on the upper part of my body. This gave me an insight that the way to help soften the body and reduce stress depended on establishing this kind of rhythmical state of the body and its mind.

What was suggested to me in this dream was a new way of behaving. I followed that suggestion exactly. I got down on my hands and knees with people and began to put my hand in the same place and do the same thing that the woman in the dream had showed me. I began to use myself in a way different than I had ever used myself. I began to re-form myself, to use my body differently, to think differently and to have other experiences. The dream suggested to me to give up standing and thinking and rolling up my eyeballs to give my thoughts the space to occur. It taught me to give up the rigidity of the observing, intellectual stance, to stop stiffening my neck and holding my breath in order to think clearly. The dream got me down on my knees, sensing the other person's body and setting up a rhythmical pattern which allowed my old rigidities to soften. It changed my body and the way I do things because I took it seriously. I literally took this dream as a model for action. That is what a dream, an image, or a feeling can do for us in middle ground: it can suggest how to use ourselves in a new way. And this is what happens sooner or later as we stay in the experiences of middle ground. We discover from within ourselves a new pattern, a new direction. We pass from the undifferentiation of middle ground when vision becomes action.

The Stage
of Formation

CONCRETIZING VISION
SOMATICALLY AND
INTERPERSONALLY

*F*ROM THE sea of middle ground, an organizing somatic current thrusts toward growth. A view forms of our situation from which we then begin to experiment with another way to use our bodies. We start to somatize our images and emotions by practicing behaviors which are involved in achieving satisfaction. We travel from the androgyny of middle ground to the differentiation of individuality. In middle ground what was discovered was something about how we want to live our life, what needs we want satisfied, how we wish to be in the world. It is a highly charged emotional experience in which we grasp certain truths about ourselves. And in the formative stage, we can make a commitment to those truths. This forming is not performing, not imitation; it is not figuring out how to do what others want us to do. It is turning insight and vision into muscle action, body shape and social form.

In the formative stages, we get ourselves ready to do something, gather ourselves together and collect our inner resources to form a new pattern of action. It requires the mobilization of images, information, and muscular patterns, to form another shape, a new way of being alive, a different body. The feelings that occur in the formative stage include both the excitement that generates the direction toward satisfaction and the feelings that accompany the steps which are involved in achieving that satisfaction. There are the feelings that come with our thinking about it, playing with it, imagining how to act, learning how to interact, and changing our associations with people.

To form new behavior requires an extended period of imagining, testing, living with failure, trying again until the behavior is mastered. It is like learning to walk or to ride a bicycle. In developing a new skill, there is awkwardness, clumsiness and hesitation as we begin. There is frustration and inadequacy until finally there is a first pattern of coordination. To successfully master the new learning then involves a period of maturation and repeated practice, the learning of nuances of feeling and movement in a variety of situations. Eventually, through time, the new skill becomes incorporated and virtually automatic.

For example, let's take a man who needs to inflate himself. His chest is both puffed up and pulled up. When he decides he no longer needs to bluff, he may have to practice bringing his chest down, and he may have to practice exhaling. He will be in a period of not knowing or deciding if he wants to be his right size. To express the new feelings that are now available to him, he may have to slow down and decrease his size and movements.

A woman has been too soft and submissive and has come to resent taking care of her husband and children. Her body begins to revolt, begins to send her desperate signals: something must end. She may become sick, get headaches and diarrhea. In middle ground, she feels lost, helpless and confused. Finally, she recognizes her need to be firm and take a stand. She begins to practice letting her jaw soften, her belly soften, and stiffening her spine, giving herself a more affirmative stance. This creates appropriate distances, which gives herself more space and others a place. It changes her identity from being a servant to being a partner.

The formative stage requires experimentation, practice and development of new ways of using ourselves, living with different feelings and responses, both in ourselves and from other people. There are a number of difficulties that people encounter in trying to form themselves.

Many of us, in our growing up, were asked to be other than we were, to follow someone else's direction, others' formative goals. Consequently, we have developed patterns that are not our own. We attempt to achieve feelings of self-worth by living from other people's values, acting on their time and doing things their way. This lack of development in our forming process can leave us with problems of impulsiveness, a feeling that life has cheated us, or a felt inability to take the necessary steps to develop a personal direction.

The organizing process can suffer from a muscular system that is weak, under-developed, that collapses, that will not or cannot sustain an assertive pattern, or only with somebody else's support. People with this pattern tend to think of themselves as losers or as cheated. There are also over-rigid types with spastic, frozen attitudes and muscles which do not expand, whose rigidity aborts their impulses, their formativeness. These and many other over-active and under-active patterns weaken the thrust of the formative process, resulting in unhappy lives.

The disruption of the formative process is not random, but reflects the way a person protects himself from real or imagined dangers; he may avoid situations, become argumentative or develop body rigidity. Or someone may maintain muscular, emotional patterns of self-inhibition such as false pride, that attitude of stiffening, elevating the head that expresses aloofness and contempt.

Perhaps, through experience, a person has developed restrictions to free expression, like stuffing his mouth to avoid crying, or the need, the readiness, to squeeze, to make himself smaller to avoid shame. In this way, the feeling life never matures, since these actions maintain a status quo, a refusal to really let the body change. Conflict is never resolved. The person has a stake in avoiding what he regards as painful experiences, like being wrong, being punished or rejected. He fears that taking risks will leave him without emotional support.

It is possible that in the past we were deflected from our course or inhibited through tragedy, maliciousness, ignorance and by our own limitations. This frustration has led to breakdown of the formative process, with all the accompanying negative feelings—i.e., anger, self-disgust, disappointment, and inferiority. Or our readiness to form a more satisfying relationship with the world may have been deflected by another's need to be stubborn, and we have developed a readiness to attack, or to withdraw or placate, to give up our goal and accept somebody else's way while trying to hold on to our own way.

So there can be a complex set of attitudes struggling for completion, or a confusion of direction. Here again, both the *How?* exercise and the accordion exercise can be beneficially employed. The *How?* enables you to experience your readiness to be defeated, or the way you handle frustration. You can, with the help of the *How?* exercise, experience and take in hand the various action patterns you employ to immobilize yourself, avoid feelings of inadequacy and inferiority and maintain your relationships with people in the old way rather than in the way that is best for you. And with the accordion you can begin to dismantle these patterns step by step, allowing the new to gradually form you.

Here is another exercise which will enable you to experience the process of forming: the exercise of kicking. D. H. Lawrence, in his book *The Psychology of the Unconscious and the Fantasia of the Unconscious,* makes a remarkable statement. He says that the child kicks its way to independence, that the child learns to use its legs as protest, and that in the exercise of using its legs as protest, it learns to become independent. It is the use of the legs and arms that teaches communication and interpendency.

The exercise of kicking can therefore help us understand, experientially, the notion of self-forming. Kicking encourages the use of the voice as well as moving the whole body into action, either as protest or as an expression of joy. Kids kick with glee. Tickle a child, and watch its legs start bouncing around. When a child is angry, he screams and his legs want to move. Then finally, it ends with jumping for joy, or stomping in a tantrum or walking away.

Lie down on your back with your shoes off. Make sure you can move and breathe easily. Now begin to kick the bed. Start with raising your legs to right angles to your body so that they go straight up in the air toward the ceiling. Then bring them straight down, hitting the bed with your heels. Keep kicking, always lifting your legs at right angles to your body. Begin to feel what the emotional experience is as well as the action.

What is the image that you have as the readiness to kick? What is the way that you kick? Is your kicking heavy? Is it light? Is your kicking in a spurt like a tantrum? Do you fatigue easily and run down? Does nothing move except your legs? Do you have to will yourself to kick, or as you begin to kick is there a natural feeling of breathing and pleasure in it?

Now, as you begin, and as you learn about your readiness-for-kicking, and as you begin to feel, what is your emotional experience of kicking and how you kick? Kicking, if it is not kicking in protest, will be rhythmical, a mixture of pleasure and assertion. Kicking has a natural focus to it, and the rhythm of the kicking has assertion, feelings of pleasure. The whole body is involved. You will notice that when the kicking becomes rhythmical, the buttocks move, the pelvis moves, the arms want to move, the whole body begins to participate in these semi-involuntary movements. Begin to kick and see what your experience is.

See, in kicking, if you don't get images and memories that are part of this experience. And as you enter into the kicking, see if you can discover an increasing amount of excitement or sensations that begin to alter your kicking. They may want to make you stop. They may want to make you kick stronger or weaker. They may want you to become elongated, with less or more breathing.

I am suggesting that as you begin to kick, you will discover that internal events — memory, excitement — begin to form the kicking into another experience, into angry kicking or despairing kicking or gleeful kicking. And it is this escalation of feeling that helps us see how we will organize our kicking differently each time. We have entered into that place where we are asked to kick not stereotypically, but to kick in response to our internal environment. Here is the challenge of forming ourselves in relationship to new messages, to a new state or attitude toward the world.

Now, stand up. Can you take the experiences you have just had kicking on the bed into the act of walking? Can you let yourself be rhythmical and assertive and pleasurable? Can you take the experiences of being voluntarily and involuntarily in your kicking action into the act of loving? Can you transfer this knowledge from the private world to the social world with your lover or with others? This is the challenge of reforming your behavior, your self, your life.

As in this experiment in kicking, the formative process gives rise to feelings of purpose. Interference with the organization of our formativeness, our satisfaction, gives rise to the distressful states we recognize as unhappiness. Its failure results in disorganization since most of us do not recognize the feeling of organization. We miss the sensations which signal breakdown and we cannot help ourselves. We flounder, we form, we deform, we are always a promise with a fear of failure. But, the more we are in contact with the feeling of our organizing process, the more responsive we are in following the direction of our own existence. Thus we can experience two patterns of action, one to reform ourselves and live out our new vision; the other to refuse ending a pattern that has meant security or safety.

It can be said that forming ourselves anew is risky. But the world is always under constant formation. We don't live in the same world we were born into, any of us. Change is going to occur whether we like it or not. It can kill us. It does kill a lot of us who can't deal with the stresses, who refuse to be reorganized.

Successfully or unsuccessfully, we live the journey of our lives, that is, the shaping and reshaping of our bodies and lifestyle. The living body, our somatic personality, is a journey and we live through its many embodiments.

In the formative process, we begin to understand that we can participate in the shaping of our lives and do not have to be victimized by change. We can grasp the nature of our experience and be faithful to it. We realize that in our lifetime we have a chance to form different bodies, different personalities. We are not stuck with being the same person throughout our entire life. This realization can be quite exciting and liberating and gives us access to the ongoing possibility of profound satisfaction.

III

Toward A Somatic Ethic

A man's correct attitude is never static; it is not something that is achieved once and for all. Rather, it is a living, moving, and changing process.

KARLFRIED, GRAF VON DURCKHEIM

Community is not an end in itself; it is a process of change.

Individual and Community

THE CHANGING SHAPES
OF RELATIONSHIPS

*A*s ONE goes through the stages of transitions, there is a cauldron of mixed emotions, feelings, and images that encourages self-discovery, being with oneself, strengthening one's privateness. But the riddle of individuality is not only in standing alone, but in commingling with others.

From the beginning, human biology is based on a faith in others and anticipated contact with them. A child has a series of internal needs which, when expressed, call forth responses that help build the emotional, somatic, and social environment that is recognized as human. The somatic connection of the child, the mother, and the father gives the excitement which makes individuality and family possible.

The concern of our culture has been the encouragement of individuality, which has been equated with being free and independent. Unfortunately, this leads to a felt polarization of "us" and "them." Actually we are always connected to others for survival as well as for satisfaction. To mature, to live one's life, does not mean to become separate, but rather to differentiate the innate talents that serve us and our community of fellow humans.

It is simply evident that societies need individuals, and individuals need society. The fallacy of the cult of individuality is the assumption that individuals stand alone. Human uniqueness lies in the process of differentiation, not polarization. It is a principle of embryology that cell differentiation is dependent upon location, position, and contact with the surrounding cells. It is the contact between cells that calls forth differentiation. The cell responds to the needs of a community of cells.

Emancipation, self-liberation, the need to be free, in the sense that is being practiced today, is often a distortion. There is really nothing free in nature. Everything is bounded; everything is connected. The contemporary idea of emancipation has really to do with power, not somatic experience. As long as emancipation is tied solely to the idea of power, people will be forced into a kind of solipsistic individualism.

Contrary to many popular psychologies, it is an illusion that feelings are exclusively private with only personal ends or that feelings, when given free expression, give rise only to individualism. And it is incorrect to say that community only comes from suppressed or hidden feelings or to conclude that individual desire and appetite must somehow be sublimated or civilized to become cultural. This is simply not the truth of human evolution.

Being able to experience and think from our process offers a resolution to the artificial conflict of individual and community. In our forming stages, for example, it is essential to reorganize our connections to our community as we reorganize ourselves somatically. We come to realize that how we are connected affects both who we are and our relationship to the community. Our private and public lives are not separated, they merge into each other. Both the shape of ourselves and the shape of the human community emerge from biological process.

In living our somatic reality we come to realize that morality, truth, beauty, love, loyalty are not experiences that have to do with ideals, but with the conditions of self-forming. From somatic experience comes the development of an ethical and moral structure that helps fulfill our unique visions as individuals and at the same time builds connections to other people. The private world of middle ground generates the capacity for cooperation and community. With the willingness to make personal visions and appetites public comes the commitment to a social reality and an openness to scrutiny and dialogue.

Out of the middle world grows the possibility of being human, of acting humanly. Coming out of the middle ground is the subjective experience of trying to make the world a reflection of the highest kinds of perceptions possible for the human being in relationship to goodness, evil, and darkness. It provides the opportunity to express the essence of all real human values that we have understood are consistent with human existence — loyalty, truthfulness, loving, being concerned. If the visions and insights of middle ground remain narcissistic, solipsistic and self-enclosed or become impersonal, objectified or emotionally uninvolved, there is a danger of being nightmarishly destructive.

We have overcome, at least in this part of the world, a lot of the "thou shalt nots." That is what psychoanalysis and modern psychology have been about. In overcoming the rigidities of a patriarchal, authoritarian world, however, we have sometimes distorted freedom and spread it thin. It comes to mean freedom to do whatever one pleases, and people are afraid to risk being called moral or developing character or restraint. What is hoisted as the supreme goal is personal power, whether it is the power of complete auton-omy to live one's life in selfish acquisition of goods and pleasure or the power to bring down established order.

The feeling of power or the search for pleasure are not the same as satisfaction or fulfillment. We need to know how to create relationships that are emotionally gratifying and how to evolve social structures that are fulfilling. This is the crisis of our time.

We have not as a society set as a goal the ability to direct our lives toward satisfaction and self-formation. To live our somatic process means to be a person in community, a person who acts in the world to develop character and satisfaction. Unlike the pursuit of power or pleasure, satisfaction presents no conflict between enhancing the public good or the family good and developing one's own feelings of goodness.

It is important that we develop a biological social ethic built upon the process of self-formation; that we learn how to build relationships that continually deepen both our individual tissue and the social fabric; and that we develop a way to live our life's urges to commingle with others in a way that is neither authoritarian, narcissistic or exploitative. When we can do this, the individual's interaction with others creates a body, an invisible body we call the social process, a body that is constantly undergoing transformation as we reorganize ourselves and our relationships.

The importance of this idea becomes clear

when we begin to look at love as a biological process. Love has often been talked about as an ideal, as a state, but rarely as a biological process that undergoes change and transformation. The deeper we live the life of our bodies, the deeper is the upwelling of love. In part, it is the recognition of others as part of the life process. What we call love is a process of how we relate our biological and social beings, how we regulate our responses, and how we make connections that give us continuity, satisfaction, and form a community. This process guarantees both individualization and human evolution.

Sexual behavior can give insight into love as a process. In sexuality, there are several endings: arousal ends the state of non-arousal; orgasm, satisfaction, ends the heightened focused pleasure. Afterwards we are in the middle ground of unbounded sensations and imagery. Here, our private worlds, our personal times, have a chance to be harmonious, to merge into unison, to develop boundaries. With these experiences, we re-enter the social world, either organizing our energies to carry the insight or experiences of the sexual connection into our working life, or to await another sexual time. From these experiences, sexuality evolves a personal loving process. Relationship, concern, sharing and knowing, join in the forming of each other. This is different from exploitation, for it recharges us and encourages growth at the cellular as well as social level, a growth of a dimension of living.

These discrete experiences build one upon the other in a pulsatory, rhythmic flow that begins to build images, pictures and tissue qualities. We begin to recognize that loving is continuous and available, that it grows and deepens. Love shapes and reshapes itself. From the history of human events, we have culled notions and experiences that are passed down, such as loyalty, the lack of exploitation, and concern. Those values are guideposts that we can incorporate into our behavior. Formed from humanity's biological experience, these traditions have value. Religious guidelines try to set up a moral structure to encourage human ways of behaving. When properly used, they are guideposts, not ideals. To set up a stereotyped image or an absolute morality, such as one should always be loyal or one should always be concerned in a very particular way, is stifling. It is so constricting that one is drowned, one is smothered in too dense a morality, just as much as one is drowned by sudden impulses without any boundaries, without having any restrictions. In the latter situation, one is over-whelmed in an ocean of unbridled impulses and desires, like a child; in the other, one is choked by a heavy load of idealistic, behavorial restrictions, in the name of love or belief. Love is either made mental and thereby idealized or stripped of cognition and made wholly lustful.

Rooted in our biology, love as a process is developmental, evolutionary, life-sustaining and promoting, pleasure-extending. We are part of a tradition that is carving our qualities of existence as humanity shapes itself, qualities of being that we call loving. Love as a process is a way of living. It is a dialogue with experience, with ourselves, and with something bigger than us. It is a dialogue with others in which we share what has been given to us.

When love is present as a process, we are urged to live our own evolution and to help others live theirs. We are willing to act with concern, to be connected, to commingle, to form community. Love, then, becomes the sharing of our biochemical abundance rather than seeking repeated remembered pleasures. It is to expand and breed new image, new possibility, to permit other persons to expand. Adding impetus to the pulsations and vibrations that are the basic phenomena that hold us and others together, loving helps us recognize that the life of the tribe, the life of the family, is in fact greater than our personal lives.

In some instances, it is the recognition that our lives, all of our lives, are insignificant. In other instances, it is the recognition that the selfish act of being individual is sometimes the greatest act of love that one can give to a community. Entering into an act with a total commitment is another face of the godhead; like the image of the warrior, it serves to show the children about being heroic, about standing and shining in one's own light, about reaching one's individuality and about living one's own body.

Previously, love, desire, was seen as an enemy of man's reasoning faculties. Uncontrolled desire hindered human development. The growth of desire, love, however, goes through phases, matures, just like any other organismic process.

Like reason, desire is a process, maturing and changing shape and expression, that can be educated. Unfortunately, the culture has seen neither love nor desire as a process. To be able to see them in this way resolves the artificial duality between love and reason, between individuality and community, and establishes a groundwork for desire, feeling, love to evolve their own process of expression from which reason grows. If the intellect can be educated, why cannot desire be educated instead of controlled?

Because we have not been educated in how to form our changing needs and desires, we come to regard with fear the natural impetus to transform ourselves and our relationships; with a lack of understanding of the formative process, we attempt to fix ourselves, to prevent change from occurring. We keep trying to recapture the state which we recognize as love. There is a particular behavior or feeling from the other person and we say: "Now my mother loves me, now my friends love me, now I feel acceptable, now that I feel I'm connected or that I can communicate with somebody, I recognize that as being in love or having love. I don't want to threaten that. I don't want to be alone because when I'm alone, I'm not loved. When I'm sent to my room, I am being punished." When we can only recognize love as a particular state, as some kind of constancy of approval or contact, we become willing to be dominated and to placate in order to perpetuate these feelings. We often develop lifestyles which make us prisoners of old needs rather than risking development and expansion.

When one finds satisfaction with another person, one of the things that happens is that more and more is demanded, not less. More is demanded out of abundance, not less. Relationships can get into trouble because satisfaction breeds a particular kind of dissatisfaction. It is the dissatisfaction that comes from satisfaction, that creates the possibility of broadening and deepening love. Most of us are taught to deal with that situation by denial. Don't want more, be thankful for what you have. But in fact, we betray ourselves if we don't recognize that satisfaction generates a demand for expanded possibilities of living.

When you can learn from your own somatic

forming, in the ways we have talked about in this book, you are enabled to accept and participate in the thrusts toward change called for by the deepening of relationships. For example, the love that I have for my five-year-old daughter, and the love that she has for me, has shaped itself and changed one hundred times over since her birth. Similarly the feelings and images that are revealed by my wife have shaped themselves, deepened, and broadened themselves in a thousand ways.

This has called for my ability to change my patterns of response, to find ways to bring new feelings into my family. As I change and as they change, the family bonds deepen and grow richer. And I can work with myself to enable these feelings to alter my other relationships, bringing different images into my work, friendships and community.

By learning about how changing excitation and feeling can make their way to new form, you are enabled to reorganize your surroundings to create deeper satisfaction. Let me give you another exercise that illustrates this process: Stand against a door or the wall, about two feet away. Reach your hands straight up to the ceiling. Then reach back and touch the wall with the palms of your hands. This will create an arch in your back like a bow so that your chest is open, and your abdomen is open and your back is stretched. If you keep your knees and your ankles bent, you will notice that the whole front of your body wants to increase its breathing.

This exercise is meant to end a contracted state in relationship to gravity, and to teach the feeling of elongating yourself. Feeling how your body elongates is entering into the middle ground. Feeling how you reorganize your stance to tolerate new ways of breathing, becomes the way of recognizing how you can stand in the world differently than you did three minutes ago.

When you take your hands down and you stand normally again, how can you find a way to transfer this feeling into dealing with people? What is the feeling? More social esteem? Being bigger, longer, more spacious? How can you transfer this into social relationships or love relationships?

The next step is to use the *How?* exercise to experience the attitudes by which you stop yourself as you begin to incorporate these new feelings into your interactions with others. Then use the accordion exercise. Perhaps you will want to return to the first exercise to again get the sense of lengthening. Then comes the period of practice, as you learned in the chapter about the Formative Stage. From this kind of experience we begin to learn about how we can respond to the changing shapes of our feelings and desires, reorganizing ourselves and our world.

This kind of work with oneself and this kind of

understanding is useful in living through the natural changes that occur in every relationship. Take for example the common situation of ending emotional dependency. In these situations, people have feelings like "I need you to support me; you need me to support you." Each of them is dependent upon the other. One has to be father or mother and the other a little girl or boy. Or they are children hiding and defending themselves against the world.

Then, for one reason or another, one person begins to bring this emotional dependency to an end. That person begins to have successes in the world, to act a little more independently. He or she begins to bring that old dependency to an end. What was not conflicting now becomes so.

This is very common. A woman begins to stop asking for support, and does not want to be stroked so much. She begins to pull back from unnecessary performing to please the man sexually or otherwise. At that moment, their relationship has begun an ending. Generally the other person responds to this with distress, with unhappiness, with fear, with complaints. Most people don't talk about it. They don't share or are unwilling to articulate their feelings because they want to protect other people's feelings. They don't want to hurt the person they are with, or they don't have the tools to say, "I don't want to be that dependent on you any longer; we have to find another way to relate." They try to go through this in the silence of their own mind figuring out what is going on with the other person and figuring out what is going on with themselves. That creates all kind of troubles including second guessing and making assumptions which may not be true. Neither person can begin to learn how to live with the changed situation emotionally and somatically. It becomes impossible to establish the kind of dialogue and practice that is necessary for both persons to reorganize the situation in a mutually satisfying manner.

When people begin to go through ending a dependency, it is better talked about or shared. The other person can begin to recognize that new distance is occurring, that the old cues are no longer there. Then that person can begin to talk about their present needs and about their own process in general terms. One doesn't have to make a psychotherapeutic melodrama out of this. One can simply talk about missed communications or an unwillingness to end dependency. Or perhaps events have progressed to the point where the other person is also able to end the dependency and they can both take that risk together. Perhaps one person will stay dependent while the other continues to become more independent. There are many shapes to living when there is emotional dialogue.

In this way, people relate to each other and

their different transitions, now able to be more with the situation of each other. People whose forming processes are at different stages don't necessarily have to separate. If one person is having an ending and the other is forming something new, they can learn from each other. It can become very interesting and exciting.

Most people don't know that going from being dependent to independent is a transitory state. It is a state that lasts a very short period of time. It is very much like that "no" state that a child has to experience when he is alienating himself from his parents. I think that what people are aiming for, is interdependency. The dependent person does not necessarily become its opposite, super-independent. The goal is not the self-made person who doesn't need anybody. We usually end up with a process of interdependence. There are times when I rely on myself and there are times when I need my family or my peers or extended family. In that sense, the real aim of changing dependency relationships is both the evolution of the individual and the formation of a functional adult community. Being super-independent is a transitory state, somewhat like middle ground.

Here again, the process of working with ourselves, being true to the changing emotional shaping of our lives, has that peculiar virtue of both encouraging individuality and establishing community, the invisible body, the social process.

111

The invisible body is the connections between people that form a living reality. There are streamers, connections of understanding, of thought, feeling, patterns of action, channels of energy, communication, contact, which is the process of community. Differentiation generates connections between people. These connections may be the encouraging of distance: "I don't want to be completely dependent upon you. I want to relate to you in a way in which I have my boundaries and you have yours. Then we breathe in and out and have a creative separation and a distance that makes me feel myself and appreciate you." But that connection between us is that invisible social body which is the strength of any family and of nations.

Being an individual takes the cooperation of many people. Communion is the union of individuals functioning as a social body that endures.

The World of Somatic Process

W HEN WE begin to work
with ourselves somatically, we participate differently with the material of our life. We become sort of an undulating river of images and sensations. Public time wanes, time becomes flexible; we have been with ourselves all day and it feels like half an hour, or we have been working with ourselves half an hour and think it has been forever. There is no sense of separation in us, and yet, we haven't lost our identity, we know who we are.

We can be so much in contact with ourselves, so much a part of our own process, that we exist for this time without need. We experience our sensations and images in such a deep way that once again we return to the same quality of being alive as in a dream, where gravity is gone. There is no up and down, image is changed and the sense of existence has been forever. Then all of a sudden we feel ourself in a dialogue or part of a process that seems to have eternity; it has no beginning or end. We seem to know something about the nature of living and our life that gives us a feeling of thankfulness and awe, in a good way, in a way which feels as if we possess faith. Our process tells us something about the act of living which makes life sweet and meaningful. Our somatic experiences ripen this feeling of universality, giving rise to faith.

In the days of old, living was not expected to be rational, predictable, or kept in order. It was an emotional experience, described in terms of destiny, fate and passion. It was not comprised of rational events like planning childhood, college or a business career. While life has become in many ways safer to live now — one isn't tortured by the demons of natural calamity or illness — we have paid an enormous price. The price that we have paid for our safety is putting in abeyance the feeling of awe and sacredness about life. Religion in the old days dealt with the experiences of the sacred, with power and with the nature of the universe or the world that we lived in. It allowed us to see our totem animal or the vision of our life, to publicly share in some very emotional life situation such as overcoming calamity, or giving thankfulness to the gods for the effulgence of the earth.

Recently, I was driving in an automobile in a flat country, the plains of Salisbury, England. I came up over a small hill that hid the plain for awhile and all of a sudden, in front of me was this huge, gigantic monolith: Stonehenge. I was awe-struck. I went closer, and I looked at those stones and I was taken back to when people shared their lives in a religious passion. That religious feeling gave them a certain feeling of being in the hands of a process bigger than they, bigger than their rationality. On the plains of Salisbury I felt con-nected to my ancestors as worshipers, builders, designers. Time had extended, elongated.

It was a feeling I recognized from working with myself somatically. And I realized then that our somatic process gives rise to the desires which are the essence of this sacred experience. In working somatically, we give up the usual boun-daries and structures, living for a time without them. We give up the known and enter the un-known, surrendering the categories which have won acceptance and recognition, and enter into the emerging impulses of love, sex, community and primordial knowing. Process both builds up and breaks down the structure of how we organize our lives, allowing, giving the possibility for im-pulses and visions to establish a religious feeling with the world around us.

The process of transition I have described gives birth to vision and helps us find ways to express that vision biologically and sociologically. Out of the great middle ground, we have the opportunity to create an ethic, a behavior that allows the body a live form of expression. The *How?* exercise is the bridge between the world of biological depth and the world of social interaction, between the sacred and the secular. It makes the sacred social.

In the new formative stages, the way things come together shows us that life is bigger than whatever we have conceived. It is an experience that restores faith in that which is bigger than us or our intellect. Something is happening, something we cannot completely control. How things come together, how things shape themselves, as every person knows, is never exactly what we expect. The very thing that happens is never quite the way that we thought about or that we would like it to be. Things come together in their own way. That is the mystery of life and the real joy of life.

Learning about our process makes the secular, mundane world also the transcendental religious universe. It makes our limited bodies a biological process, a universal limitless experience. We are the life process on the planetary and cosmological levels. In possessing a deepened awareness and an expanded experience of us as an ongoing process, we become explorers, participants able to live many viewpoints, knowing there are multiple dimensions of truth, of world view and human nature. Once we begin to experience living as process, we will see the possibility for living and forming our lives — not as slaves or victims, but as pioneers.

Man has gone through the stages of being a victim to nature, then dominating nature, and now trying to cooperate with nature. We have gone through the stage of trying to understand ourselves in relationship to the world, then how to understand ourselves, and now how to work with ourselves. That is what we are dealing with here: the forming of human beings; not changing the outer environment, but, in fact, changing our internal environment. This requires that we learn to recognize different muscle states. It requires learning to differentiate the energy states, the organ movements with their pulsatory quality of tight or soft, the qualities of our hunger. It is the recognition of these organic states, the feel of our insides, the language of the intestines, which give us the information we need to live better.

I have tried to show that an attitude, a like or a dislike, a mental concept, a relationship or an emotional set, are all based upon physical, muscular, postural action patterns. These can be changed, must be changed, if we are to change our lifestyles in a deeply satisfying way.

I believe the notion and the experience of our lives, as process, opens the door for a new vision of human beings. The human being is not a fixed entity, not an image of perfection or a creature doomed to resolve conflict or live in duality, swinging between light and dark, good and evil, rational and irrational, sacred and secular. You will notice that there are many kinds of phenomena in process—rational, irrational, emotional, cognitive, sensation and image, objectifying, subjectifying, social, private; all connected, all a part of the living of life.

We are a biological life process that thinks, feels, has needs, is able to have highly specialized responses, able to dream and to act. We are a chain of events, an entire ecological system with many life environments, from tidal pools and ancient biochemical seas to highly complex, brain-organ action systems. We are continually on the move, continually forming, reorganizing ourselves and our surround. By living from our process, we can commit ourselves to the evolution of the living, the forming of the self, the culture, the planet. We can form ourselves rather than live from inappropriate images.

A person who is process-oriented can live with situations. That doesn't mean that he is an opportunist. It does mean that he doesn't have to impose ideals, dogma, or categories on situations, but can be alive with what is growing, maturing and ripening. A process person doesn't need rigid mental emotional models. He can think without them, or feel without them. This person can be alive responsively and self-generatingly. He knows that life doesn't need to speak logically,

that he can live with an intuitive or feeling knowing. A process person is a citizen of many realms
of existence in the public and private worlds. He is
willing to unlearn, to create new realities and
willing to recognize the unconditioned.

A process person asks not too many why's,
but a lot of how this is going on. How am I
involved? How am I doing it? How am I ending?
How am I pausing? How am I forming? What is
going on, how am I in it, with it, doing it? How is
my life, my time, and how do I seek expression
and satisfaction?

He knows that to be able to change, to let ourselves be different throughout our lifetime, is not
to dominate ourselves, not to be dominated by
our impulses. Nor is it to control ourselves, our
emotions, or force ourselves to perform. It is not
to exploit ourselves, always demanding a profit
for our giving. He knows that to let ourselves
reorganize ourselves is our challenge, that
forming-reforming transcends the given for more
heightened satisfaction. It is the delight of living.

Working with process deepens pleasure, con-
cretizes potential, generates living styles and
environments. That is the process way of organizing experience — forming, passion, desire. It
makes distinctions between instinctual and
human behavior, between determinism and
open-endedness, between fixed absolutism and
participatory evolution.

Being with ourselves somatically, we are faced with two ethical choices. One is to remain faithful to our own experience, and the other is the public demand. But in experiencing our own process of forming, we find our inner life, our emotions and our passions. Morality, truth, beauty, love, and loyalty are not fixed ideals, but experiences that spring from our own life thrust. We realize that we are a web of life that is interdependent and that living our individuality is a gift to our society, a loyalty to what is forming.

We are thereby enabled to fulfill the nature of our own experiences, to live our individuality and community, and to live the changing forms of the movement of our lives.

CENTER FOR ENERGETIC STUDIES

The Center for Energetic Studies, under the direction of Stanley Keleman, seeks to structure a modern contemplative approach to self-knowing and living in which one's own subjective process gives birth to a set of values which then guides the whole of one's life. Today's values are increasingly divorced from our deepest processes, and bodily experience has been misunderstood and relegated to second place.

Somatic reality is an emotional reality that is much larger than innate genetic patterns of behavior. Emotional reality and biological ground are the same and cannot, in any way, be separated or distinguished. Biological ground also means gender, the male and female responses that are innate to human life, the sexual identity with which we are born. Somatic reality is at the very core of existence, the source of our deepest religious feelings and psychological perceptions.

Classes and programs at the Center offer a psycho-physical practicum that brings to use the basic ways a person learns. The key issue is *how* we use ourselves—learning the language of how viscera and brain use muscle to create behavior. These classes teach the essential somatic aspect of all roles and dramatize the possibilities of action to deepen the sense of connection to the many worlds in which all of us participate.

For further information, write to:
Center for Energetic Studies
2045 Francisco Street
Berkeley, California 94709